Walking *through* the Valley of the Shadow of Death

Walking *through* the Valley of the Shadow of Death

Kathryn Cunningham

CFI
An imprint of Cedar Fort, Inc.
Springville, Utah

Paperback ISBN 13: 978-1-4621-4718-2
eBook ISBN 13: 978-1-4621-4779-3

Published by CFI, an imprint of Cedar Fort, Inc.
2373 W. 700 S., Suite 100, Springville, UT 84663
Distributed by Cedar Fort, Inc., www.cedarfort.com

Library of Congress Cataloging Number: 2024931624

Cover design by Shawnda Craig

Edited by Liz Kazandzhy

Printed in the United States of America

10 9 8 7 6 5 4 3 2 1

Printed on acid-free paper

For my loving husband and three incredible daughters.
Thank you for walking through the valley with me.

Contents

1
Shadows in the Valley

The first time I lived in a valley was when I attended college at Brigham Young University, a Church-owned school nestled in the Utah Valley. The mountains that surround the campus to the east and west are gorgeous, and I grew to love their constant companionship during my time there. Of course, there is a downside to living in a valley. With the beauty of the mountains comes the cold and darkness of their shadow. I felt it in the unseasonably sharp bite in the air on my morning walks to school. And I saw it in the sudden blackness of winter evenings when I forgot the danger and studied too late at the library.

Twenty years after I graduated from college, my family moved to another valley in Utah, the Tooele Valley. My son loved to ride his bike around the neighborhood in the afternoons, and all too often the cold and dark of the mountain's shadow crept up on him before he remembered to come home. I would have to go fetch him because the short ride back to our house had become dangerous.

Living in a valley means negotiating the consequences of the mountain's shadow. The shadow changes how you experience your day and makes you reevaluate how you live your life and how you protect your children. It changes how you see the world.

The scriptures tell us of a different sort of valley, surrounded by a mountain as immutable and inescapable as any we find in the natural world. "Yea, though I walk through the valley of the shadow of death, I will fear no evil" (Psalm 23:4).

Death. It looms over us from the day we are born until the day it overtakes us. We live our lives in its shadow. Some try to keep it at a distance. Some even try to run away from it. But it will always be there, just over your shoulder, as long as you are in this world. Being alive means negotiating the consequences of death.

Like a mountain, death can be beautiful—the end of a life of pain and sorrow and a return to loved ones long departed. It is proof that God loves us and that He has a plan that is not limited by the confines of this world but stretches out from eternity to eternity. But it is also terrible, a towering edifice of loss and grief that can crush your breath and obliterate your sanity with ease. When death's shadow finds you standing on a sandy foundation, you will feel the earth turn to quicksand under your feet and you will be sucked down under an endless wave of anger and despair.

It's dangerous living in the valley. And we don't know how long our journey through it will be. All we really know is that every step forward brings us closer to the mountain. How do we walk through this valley without being afraid, as the Psalmist declares? How do we negotiate the consequences of the shadow and still find ways to be touched by the sun?

There must be a way.

I know there is a way.

He is the Way.

2
The Shadow Falls

"Mrs. Cunningham, can you come to the school immediately?"

"What happened?"

"Dallin fell off the slide at recess. He's unresponsive."

"I'll be right there."

* * *

It was a regular, unremarkable Monday morning. I had spent the weekend trying to finish up some paperwork—a federal disability retirement application—for my husband Tim. I was about to go to the post office to mail it off when I got the call from the school. The shadow of death fell quickly and suddenly over my family. We never saw it coming.

Dallin is my youngest child and my only boy. I grew up in a family of sisters, and the six of us were quite proud of our little sorority. We never felt the need to be rescued by a man. When there was furniture to be moved or grass to be mowed or a problem to be solved, we did it ourselves. Most men we knew were a bit inferior to the women in our lives—certainly they couldn't hold a candle to our father—and we looked on them with more than a little disdain. We never wished for a brother to break up our close-knit sisterhood. So when I found out my fourth child would be a boy, it took some time for me to get excited about it.

But life grows inside you and changes the way you look at yourself and the world. And the day I held my son in my arms and asked him what his name should be, I knew he was sent to complete our family. We needed him just as much as he needed us.

Our Dallin.

When my husband and I got to the school and saw the first responders performing chest compressions on our son—his tiny eight-year-old stomach heaving up every time they pushed down on his chest, trying desperately to force his heart to start beating again—I had to look away. I knew what was happening, yet I didn't believe it. I couldn't believe it. It was like stepping into a nightmare you expect to be able to wake up from. It shouldn't be possible, and yet it was happening right in front of me.

They took Dallin to the local emergency room where they got his heart beating again. Then they rushed him to Primary Children's Hospital in Salt Lake City, hoping the doctors there would be better equipped to assess and treat his condition. But his injuries were too severe. In every meaningful sense of the word, Dallin's life had ended out on that playground. It was impossible for him to recover. On Tuesday evening, we finally told them to turn off the machines and we let him go. And we listened to a very kind doctor utter the most horrible words a parent can hear.

"I'm very sorry to tell you that Dallin has died."

3
Expect the Miracle

I AM A RELIGIOUS PERSON, AND IN TIMES OF TRAGEDY, RELIGIOUS PEOple are fond of saying, "Everything happens for a reason." I don't want to make anyone feel bad who has said this to me—and if this phrase gives you comfort, I don't want to take that away from you either—but I don't think those words are quite right. I don't think they tell the whole truth. They imply that God is causing bad things to happen to us—that He planned it all out and made it happen for the sake of His eternal lesson plan. And that's just not true. God didn't push Dallin off that slide. He wasn't lying in wait for the perfect moment to nudge him over the edge at just the right angle so that his head would hit the frozen ground and his brain would be damaged beyond repair. God didn't kill my son. Not for a million good reasons would He be capable of such a thing.

God is our Father. And He sent us out into a world that is dangerous and unpredictable, knowing that sometimes bad things will happen to us. I am a mother. And every day I send my sweet children out into a world that is dangerous and unpredictable, knowing that sometimes bad things will happen to them. As parents, why do we do this? Why don't we lock the doors, bar up the windows, and encase our children in a world that is only love, only safety, only protection? Why do we put them through it? Why do we take the risk?

We do it, of course, because we love them. We know they can't have a full life locked in a basement. We know they can't become their best, truest selves if they never leave the house, no matter how much love and attention we give them. Everything worth having requires a risk, and we take that risk so our children can truly live. It's the same with our Heavenly Father.[1]

Of course, the difference between us as parents and God as a parent is that He is all-powerful. The scriptures are full of stories where God intervenes miraculously in the lives of His children. In The Church of Jesus Christ of Latter-day Saints, we teach that those miracles continue today. "God hath not ceased to be a God of miracles," the scriptures say (Moroni 9:15). Our prophet, President Russell M. Nelson, said to us recently in a worldwide meeting of the Church that we should "seek and expect miracles."[2] The day before Dallin's accident, people at church couldn't seem to stop quoting that talk. I kept hearing it mentioned over and over from so many people that I went home that day convinced that the Holy Ghost had brought that phrase to my attention on purpose. I wrote in my journal about it that night. I had all kinds of theories about what God wanted me to learn and what He might be preparing me for.

The next day, I stood on the elementary school playground, praying for a miracle.

When the EMTs drove Dallin from the school to the local hospital in an ambulance, my husband and I were not allowed to ride with him. On the short drive to the ER, my mind began to splinter. Fragmented thoughts of what might have been done differently and what might be coming in the future flashed across my brain. I knew that if I gave space to any of those thoughts, I would fall apart and be useless. I had to focus on the present. I had to keep an iron grip on my mind and only allow myself to think about exactly what was going on right then, at each moment as it came. More than one moment would be too much, and I would become hysterical. To help maintain my focus, I repeated

---

1. See Larry Richman, "Learning through Life's Trials" (Brigham Young University–Idaho devotional, Oct. 30, 2007), byui.edu.

2. Russell M. Nelson, "The Power of Spiritual Momentum," *Liahona*, May 2022, 99.

President Nelson's words to myself, over and over, holding tight to the promise made to me by a prophet of God.

"I will expect the miracle. I will expect the miracle. I know You, Lord. I know what You can do. I will expect the miracle."

I think I knew even then that the miracle I wanted was not the miracle I was going to receive.

Dallin did not rise miraculously from his deathbed. He died. And when he did, we had a choice. We could believe that the promise of miracles had gone unfulfilled and that our faith in Jesus Christ and all the prophets of the ages was a lie—a scam more devious and destructive than any the world has ever known. There was a moment when I sat with my son's hand in mine and considered that possibility. It was just a flash—the stroke of a laser across my thoughts—but it was there and I saw it. And I looked at my dying son and knew I would never choose it. I would take the other option. I gripped his hand even more tightly and promised him that I would never doubt, that I would always believe, that I would never do anything that put our eventual reunion in jeopardy. I would choose the path of faith because it was the path that had given me strength in the past, and it is the only path that can save me going forward. I would keep seeking and expecting miracles, not in spite of this tragedy but because of it.

The miracle of the gospel of Jesus Christ is not that we are spared the pain of grief and tragedy if we believe in Him. The miracle is that if we soften our hearts and have faith in Him, Jesus Christ will take the worst moments of our lives, the ones that should break us, and transform them, refine them, and forge them into the steel that will make us unbreakable. He is the artist who created the world from "matter unorganized." He can take the raw materials of our broken hearts and create a work of art in our souls—a mosaic of understanding, wisdom, compassion, love, and even peace. As we read in 2 Timothy 1:7, He will give us a spirit "of power, and of love, and of a sound mind." These gifts will make us our best and truest selves. They will teach us what it means to truly live.[3]

---

3. See Dallin H. Oaks, "Strengthened by the Atonement of Jesus Christ," *Ensign* or *Liahona*, Nov. 2015, 61–64.

These are the miracles we seek. We rise every morning expecting to find them. And we do. I can't tell you all the miracles that you will receive as you bravely put one foot in front of the other on your journey through the valley of the shadow of death. But I can tell you about some of mine.

4

The Miracle of Peace

When Tim and I pulled into the elementary school parking lot that Monday, the ambulance was already on the scene. We learned later that someone from the sheriff's department was actually the first to arrive and take over CPR from the school's recess monitor. Tim went right over to Dallin, standing near his head and closely observing the activities of the first responders. His job requires him to conduct investigations—to gather and analyze evidence and put together timelines. I think his way of coping with the situation was to follow this same investigative process for piecing together what was happening to his son. He had to be close to the action, documenting it, analyzing it, filing away unanswered questions for later. I hung back. I knew I had to deal with the situation, but I didn't have any experience with this kind of emergency or the violence that was being inflicted on Dallin's body. I couldn't be close to it—couldn't take it in all at once.

The principal came over and put an arm around me, trying to give a brief explanation of what happened. She was new to the job this year, so she didn't know me, but she was kind and I could tell she cared about the kids. A couple of the staff who did know me (from all the times I substitute taught the year before) came over to give me hugs and words of support. I was grateful for their sympathy and heartfelt sorrow, but I could only hear so much of it. All of my mental energy was focused on the very intense inner dialogue I was conducting with the Lord.

"Please save Dallin's life, Heavenly Father. Please help him be okay. Please bless the first responders to know what to do to save him. Make his heart start beating again, Father. I know you can do it. Please help us."

I said the words, but I was empty inside. I had faith in Jesus, but I had no idea what to hope for. My heart didn't know how to feel, so I didn't feel anything. I have spent my life trying to figure out how to communicate with God, and I believe I have gotten a reasonably good handle on what it usually feels like when He's speaking to me. Most of the time when I reach out to Him, I at least feel a nudge in response—an acknowledgment that He's listening and that He cares about what I'm going through. On this day, as I stood on the playground pleading with Him to intervene, heaven was unresponsive.

Then there was a moment when everyone had withdrawn from me, and I could whisper a few words to God out loud without sounding like a crazy person.

"Father, if Thou wilt, save my boy."

I felt a very profound peace deep in my heart. It washed over me and then it was gone. It was fleeting and tender and fragile, but it was enough to reassure me that I was not alone.

So often, the peace God sends us is like this. He can't make empty promises, and He won't save us from suffering that is essential to our human experience. But He will sit with us in our extremities. I'm grateful that God was straightforward with me when I begged for the things I wanted but that He knew He wasn't going to give me. I'm grateful He was silent for a time—that He didn't underestimate me or coddle me in those first mind-numbingly horrible moments. If He had responded right away, I might have set my heart on the wrong miracle and not been in the correct mindset to see all the miracles He was sending me along the way.

Heavenly Father sees into our minds and our hearts, and He waits for the right time to send us peace. For me, it was when I was still, when I was alone, when I could really talk to Him and wouldn't misunderstand the message He was sending me. He was not going to save me from the awfulness of those two days, and Dallin would not be spared an early death. But God *would* save my boy. At the end of the nightmare, He would bring him safely home. And He would go with me into the darkness of the shadow, giving me eyes to see and helping me find my way.

5
The Miracle of Priesthood

Before I went to college, I had never lived in Utah. My parents were both born and raised in southern California, so I don't have any close family connections there. And there aren't many Navy bases in landlocked states, so my dad's military career never took us there either. As a lifelong, committed member of The Church of Jesus Christ of Latter-day Saints, I developed a sense of pride in my non-Utah-ness. I valued the diversity of the people I met in the various places I lived, and I felt I understood my faith better because I was exposed to a wide variety of ideas and perspectives in my schools and neighborhoods. I never experienced the pressures of subversive culture or tradition that so easily grow up alongside the doctrine of a church and entangles itself like tares among the wheat in the communities where a single religion is the predominant force.

I admit to thinking myself a bit superior to "Utah Mormons" for most of my young life. I've spent a lot of time repenting for that prideful attitude as an adult. Many of my dearest friends were born and raised in Utah, and they have taught me not to be so judgmental. But it was still a big mental shift when I moved to the Tooele Valley in my forties and had to start thinking of myself as being "from Utah" now.

Having said all that, I have to say that one of the nice things about living in Utah for a member of the Church is that there is always someone on hand who knows what you need when you need it, religiously speaking. You can make a request or get a thing done without giving a twenty-minute sermon on the historical background or doctrinal significance of the thing. Someone will be there who understands what you need and why it's so important to you. This is especially true with regards to priesthood blessings in times of emergency.

When Tim and I arrived at the emergency room of our small local hospital, Dallin's room was a flurry of activity. An attendant got chairs for us, and we attempted to stay close by without getting in anybody's way. As soon as they got Dallin's heart beating again, the staff began prepping him for transport to Primary Children's Hospital in Salt Lake City. Normally he would have been life-flighted, but weather conditions weren't conducive to air travel, so they were going to have to use an ambulance. There wasn't room for us to ride along.

I was anxious for them to be on their way, but I was also worried that they would load him up before we had a chance to give him a priesthood blessing. If I was going to be seeking and expecting miracles, I knew we needed the power of the priesthood on our side. And there is something about exercising the faith to make time for a blessing when there isn't even a second to spare that opens the windows of heaven. I wanted those windows wide open.[4]

I tried to look for a person I could speak to about it, but everyone was, understandably, quite preoccupied with doing their job. I also knew that Tim, though he was a worthy priesthood holder, was not in the habit of carrying consecrated oil with him at all times.[5] The creases in my forehead deepened as I tried to figure out what to do.

Mercifully, an ER doctor came to us with a pitcher of consecrated oil (yes, a pitcher—apparently they give a lot of blessings in the emergency room) and offered to assist Tim in giving Dallin a blessing before the ambulance got underway. The doctor anointed Dallin with the oil and Tim sealed the anointing, offering the shortest of blessings. I wasn't near enough to hear what was said, but I could see Tim's face contort with emotion and noticed moisture form at the corner of his

---

4. See Dallin H. Oaks, "Healing the Sick," *Ensign* or *Liahona*, May 2010, 47–50.

5. For those who don't know, consecrated oil is used to give special blessings of healing to those who are sick or have been injured. You can still give a blessing without the oil, but it's not quite the same (See James 5:14).

eyes. He told me later that he remembers saying, "Whether you live or die, continue to be a strength and comfort to your family." Quite an admonition for an eight-year-old fighting for his life. As for me, when I saw Tim give that blessing, I felt a weight lifted from my shoulders along with another sustaining wave of peace from the Lord.

For some, that series of events is pretty unremarkable, especially since, in the end, it doesn't seem to have changed anything. But for me, it was a miracle. I could move forward with what I had to do knowing that although Dallin would be going in that ambulance without us, he would not be going alone. The power of the priesthood would go with him. I would never have to wonder how things would have turned out if only we had found a way to give him that blessing before he left. We had done all we could for our son's healing, and now we had to leave it in the hands of God and the doctors.

Now, of course, knowing the words that Tim spoke, my perspective of the miracle of that blessing has broadened. I believe it was a miracle for Dallin as well as for me, because whether he was still in his body or hovering nearby, he heard it. I think the things Tim said under the influence of the Spirit and as an authorized servant of the Lord helped Dallin have a sense of purpose during those hours of limbo when his body wasn't functional but his spirit was still tied to this world. Come life or come death, he knew he had service to give and a mission to fulfill. I certainly felt Dallin reaching out to me to give me strength and comfort while he was in the hospital, and I'm sure there were others who felt it too. But I also believe he carried that purpose with him when it was time for him to leave this life. His final priesthood blessing is a reminder to him and to us that the ties that bind us are stronger than death—that we continue to strengthen and comfort each other from a distance even when the mountain divides us from one another. And we will continue to do so until we are together again.

When the blessing had been given and the doctors resumed prepping Dallin for transport, Tim and I left the hospital. As quickly as we could, we picked up our daughters from their various schools and got a neighborhood friend to stay with them until my sister could make it over from her house in Orem about an hour away. Then we were off to Primary Children's.

Another of my sisters, who was the Relief Society president in her congregation in California, found a way to get my bishop's contact information and updated him on the situation. He dispatched a member of our congregation to meet Tim and me at the hospital to give us priesthood blessings. He was waiting for us in the front lobby when we arrived. It all happened behind the scenes, without us having to spare a thought or lift a finger.

The front desk receptionist at Primary Children's called a nurse from the Pediatric Intensive Care Unit (PICU) down to escort us to Dallin's room. We asked her if she had a place where our dear friend could give us a blessing before we went up. Again, we didn't have to give an explanation, and we didn't have to ask twice. She understood what we needed, found an empty room, and waited patiently for us to be done.

I don't remember what was said in the blessing that was given to me, but I do remember feeling comforted by it. Tim's blessing was more remarkable.

My husband's family has a complicated backstory involving multiple weddings, affairs, and divorces. One of the things I admire most about them is how they have managed to make their peace with their situation and see themselves as part of one large family in spite of past hurts and regardless of whether the ties that bind them are from nature or nurture. It's one of the reasons I fell in love with Tim so quickly. Every time he learned about a new twist or turn along the winding path of his genealogy, Tim would take it in stride and say, "Just one more person to love." The details of all this are irrelevant to this story, except to say that Tim's biological father, Greg, is not the father he was raised by. That's Max.

Max died about five years ago after a sudden heart attack. It was a real blow to all of his family. Max was a good and tender man who experienced quite a bit of heartbreak in his life. All of his children love him to pieces. One of the hardest things that ever happened to Max was losing his firstborn son when he was just an infant. Well, when our sweet friend placed his hands on Tim's head, Tim immediately felt Max in the room. It was as if Max's hands were on his head, giving him that blessing. Max's arms were around him, holding him and lifting him up.

Max knew what it was to lose a son, and now so would Tim. This ordeal would be yet another thing they would share—an experience that would bond father to son in life and into eternity. The power of the priesthood had opened the windows of heaven, and an angel had come through them. Max would stay with my husband. As Jesus was prepared to succor us "according to our infirmities" by taking "upon him the pains and sicknesses of his people" (Alma 7:11–12), Max was prepared to succor his son by enduring great suffering during his mortal life. He was ready when Tim needed him, and because Tim was seeking miracles, it was easy for them to find each other.

We don't have to be alone in the shadow. It is dark in the valley when the shadow descends, but when we go in expecting the miracle, there will be angels who will walk with us and stay with us when we need them most. The Lord will open our eyes, as He did for the servant of Elisha, and we will behold that "the mountain [is] full of horses and chariots of fire round about [us]" (2 Kings 6:17). They will light our path and defend us from the powers that would destroy us.

6
The Miracle of Preparation

AFTER TIM AND I RECEIVED OUR BLESSINGS, THE NURSE TOOK US UP to the PICU. There, a very kind and sensitive doctor sat us down and spoke to us about Dallin's condition. He talked about how long Dallin had undergone chest compressions and the inability of the brain to withstand that length of time with little to no oxygen flow. In hindsight, it's all too clear that this doctor was attempting to very gently let us know that Dallin was essentially dead—that his body was past the point of recovery. Tim and I are both very educated and insightful people—realistic people with experience in both communication and the reality of death—and we should have gotten the message. But we just weren't ready to understand what he was telling us. It would take time for us to be willing to know what we didn't want to know.

Eventually, that initial conversation did sink in, and it helped me ask the questions and make the connections I needed in order to make the right decision for Dallin. I recognize now that it was easier to accept what I had to do in the end because the doctor tried his best to prepare me from the beginning.

As I consider the events of my life, it has become clear to me that God had spent decades preparing me to meet this moment.

He didn't let me in on exactly what He was preparing me for, obviously. If I had known when I first held Dallin that he would be with us for just eight brief years, the sorrow of what was to come would have been all I could see. It would have tainted every joyful moment we had together, and I wouldn't have cherished the time we were given because it would have been overshadowed by the knowledge of what we would suffer in the future. So God let me raise my son in blissful ignorance. He gifted me precious time free from the weight of worry and fearful anticipation.

Yet like our kind doctor, the Great Physician of mankind took every opportunity to prepare me to know what I didn't want to know. He layered my life with experiences and knowledge that prepared me for what He knew was coming. And then, when I asked for a miracle, He gave me eyes to see the grand design woven into the fabric of my life. He has been with me in every detail, at every crossroad, at every step, ensuring that when this day came, I would have the tools I needed to get through it. The miracle I needed had been a lifetime in the making. It was ready when I needed it. I just had to seek it.

Just a few examples will suffice to illustrate my point.

My Father

It took my dad a while to figure out what he wanted to be when he grew up. As a result, he was in his thirties and had five kids when he graduated medical school. I was number three, and I can just barely remember sitting in the audience, watching him walk across the stage to receive his diploma. He was the only graduate with a fan club of tiny girls screaming, "Yay Daddy!"

After graduation, he began work as a pediatrician. He also spent considerable time, energy, and money getting a specialty within that field: pediatric oncology/hematology (children's cancers and blood diseases). He only practiced in his specialty for a few years, but they were formative years for me, and they had a profound impact on my developing mind and heart.

My dad didn't leave his work at work, not entirely. Without violating patient confidentiality, he talked to us about his work. It was quite normal for us to sit around the dinner table discussing his patients: how young some of them were, how sick they got from both their illness and the medicines they had to take, how hard my dad worked to save them, and how there were many who he just couldn't save.

He didn't hide the injustice of it from us. It isn't ever fair that a child gets cancer. There is no "why" sufficient to explain it. It is simply and always a horrible tragedy. But it is real. No amount of "kicking against the pricks" (Acts 9:5) will change it. The only productive thing to do is accept it, evaluate it, and do what you can to fight it. And sometimes you lose that fight.

I remember my dad talking to us about his patients who died. He described to us the hard decisions that parents have to make when it's clear the cancer has won the war and that further treatment will only cause additional pain and suffering. I saw how difficult it was for him to have to have those conversations with parents. I saw how difficult it was for parents to make the merciful choice to discontinue treatment. And I saw how the pain of it was relieved significantly by the knowledge that life and families continue on after the death of this body.

In the safety of those family discussions, I learned what it means to accept the fragile mortality of our bodies yet truly believe in the immortality of the soul through the Atonement of Jesus. "For as in Adam all die, even so in Christ shall all be made alive" (1 Corinthians 15:22). I saw the mountain, and I learned not to be afraid of it. I learned the difference between abandoning all hope in the face of tragedy versus calmly, logically, and lovingly recognizing the truth that the data are showing you and choosing to spend your final moments with your child in peace. I came to admire and respect the parents who had the strength and love to make that hard decision.

My dad thought he took on his specialty to help his patients and their families. And he did. His work as a pediatric oncologist changed the lives of everyone around him for the better, and the experience he gained has made him a more effective doctor throughout his career as a much-beloved pediatrician. But it also helped me be ready when the time came for me to see with clear eyes and make an impossible choice for the love of my child.

The Lord is a master of efficiency. When we follow the path He chooses for us, He miraculously consecrates our work and our experience in order to bless the lives of the maximum number of people possible. Our efforts to follow God's will for us will affect our children for good in ways we could not have anticipated. My dad could not have known I would lose a child. But he chose a career that the Holy Ghost prompted him to choose. He used what he experienced in that career to teach us eternal truths at every opportunity he got. And thirty years later, those teachings turned out to be exactly what I needed.

I am grateful to my Heavenly Father for leading my dad, and I am grateful to my dad for being the kind of man who was willing to be led by Him.

Shortly after Dallin died, I went into my garage, probably to take the trash out, and found my dad there. He was tenderly placing Dallin's helmet back onto the handle of his bike. It must have fallen on the ground when someone bumped into it. We were always tripping over Dallin's bike. But he rode it so often, it didn't make any sense to put it neatly in a corner where it would be out of the way. I could see by the look in his eyes and the trembling of his hands that Dallin's death was affecting my dad differently than any of his patients' deaths—more than the death of his parents or even that of his sister. Something about this one had shaken him.

Later, I had the opportunity to talk to him about it. I thanked him for teaching me the gospel, the power of faith, and the salvation of Jesus. And I thanked him for being honest with me about things he knew would be hard for a young person to understand. Like the Lord, he didn't coddle or underestimate me. He told me the truth, and in doing so, he taught me to face the mountain without fear.

"I was prepared because you prepared me."

My dad and I knew we would have a hard time making our way through the shadow, but we would do it together and come through in the strength of the Lord.

Married Life

Following college and missionary service, I decided to study French translation and interpretation in Monterey, California. My first Sunday there, a strapping young man caught my eye at church. Tim was fresh out of Army basic training, studying Korean at the Defense Language Institute just up the hill from my little graduate school. He was strong, smart, shy, and funny. I lost my heart to him on our very first date, walking for miles along the beach talking about our lives and interests.

We got married about three months later, and our first child was born nine months after that.

Whenever people get married so quickly, without a real chance to get to know the finer points of each other's personalities, there are bound to be problems. We had our share. Every challenge that we met and overcame strengthened our relationship, but they also whittled away at my assumption that I would have any kind of control over the course my life would take.

We had been married less than two years when we found ourselves stationed in South Korea. During our year there, Tim injured his back, I had a miscarriage, and I had my first ever seizure and was consequently diagnosed with epilepsy. Then I suffered dramatic mental and emotional turmoil due to the side effects of the many seizure medications we went through trying to find one that worked for me. After that, the Army sent us to Germany where I immediately had another miscarriage. I was thrown into a deep and profound depression and spent the next four years finding my way through it.

Depression found me again several years later. Tim's back injury had become so severe that he had ended his military service and was working to get his master's degree at the same graduate school I had been going to when we met. We had four children and were living in a two-bedroom apartment. For years, I had been working under the belief that Tim's disabilities were confined to his back. I knew that he experienced anxiety and depression, but I had assumed that these would diminish and then disappear as he spent more time away from his military job. I thought he would be like he was before. I was wrong.

When I was finally forced to recognize that these mental and emotional disabilities were permanent—that Tim would never get better, only worse—it broke me. I was thrown into a depression so crippling that I often went to bed thinking how nice it would be if I didn't wake up in the morning. I was never suicidal; I was never tempted to take action to end my life myself. But the idea that your problems could just be magically whisked away through the intervention of a higher power is intoxicating when you're broken. It takes extreme discipline not to entertain that fantasy.

In the end, God did not take the matter out of my hands. I kept getting out of bed every day for the people who needed me. I learned, slowly and with help, to accept my husband as he was and my situation as it was, and eventually I found myself looking forward to the sunrise again.

Just as I felt myself beginning to heal, another series of events took control of my life away from me. Tim had graduated with a master's degree and gotten a job in Fairfax, Virginia. I loved it there and was making plans to stay for many years. But then Tim's dad, Max, and his older sister, DeLynn, died in quick succession, and we realized how many other relatives we had who were in poor health. With Max gone, Tim felt a responsibility to take on a stronger leadership role in his family, nearly all of whom live in northern Utah. We couldn't afford to make the cross-country drive from Virginia to Utah every time someone died or needed our help. We had to be closer.

So Tim took a job in Henderson, Nevada. We bought a house for the first time. We discussed how such an investment warranted staying put for at least five years. I made plans to stay.

Then COVID hit; Tim's biological father, Greg, died; and Tim's health began to get worse at a dizzying pace. Toward the end of quarantine, he was driving the six hours to Utah once a month or so to help various family members, and the stress of those constant commutes was taking an additional toll on his health. We began discussing another premature move.

This time my heart fought back. My prayers became complaining sessions.

"Heavenly Father, I don't want to move again. I shouldn't have to. We had a plan; I just want to do it the way we planned. I'm so, so angry, and I just don't want to."

In a rare moment of direct communication from God, an answer came to my mind one night as I ranted. "It doesn't matter what you want. This decision isn't about you."

It was a hard pill to swallow. It's never easy to be told by someone you love that what you want isn't important. It stings. But my heart reassured me that the issue wasn't that God didn't *care* about what I wanted or how I felt. He always cares—He's my father. It's just that what I wanted was irrelevant to the decision we had to make. As soon as I heard it, I knew it was true. So I softened my heart, put what I wanted aside, and tried to focus on what was right. We moved to Utah.

Now, I'm not writing all this to whine about my hard life. It's been quite an easy life compared to many whose stories I've known. And I'm not writing it to show how unselfish and self-sacrificing I am. I can't even put those words on paper without chuckling a little at the idea. The point of this long sob story is to show how carefully and mercifully the Lord prepared me to meet this day.

Some people need to learn to hold tight and stand strong in the face of soul-crushing tragedy. I had to learn to let go. If I hadn't spent years gradually learning to let go of the idea that I could will my way into good health and predictable outcomes for myself and my husband, I would have been decimated when death came for my son. I had to learn to bend with the winds of adversity, and God showed me how. It was painful. I didn't like it. I wouldn't choose it, just like I wouldn't have chosen this. But it was what I needed, and God knew it.

Now, some insightful readers will note that if we had done what I wanted and stayed in Virginia or Nevada, Dallin would probably still be alive. That may be true. Then again, maybe not. The dangers of this world are so unpredictable. We can't know for sure what would or wouldn't have happened if we had done certain things differently. There were a million reasons why moving to Utah was the right thing to do. I don't regret it. And I'm grateful that an omniscient Father in Heaven used that experience as an opportunity to instruct my mind and change my heart in the exact ways I needed.

Because of Jesus, the things that should have broken me made me unbreakable.

That is the miracle.

Future

As I reflect on what great pains the Lord has taken to prepare me for the death of my son, I can't help but wonder (with more than a little trepidation) what future events this tragedy might be preparing me for. It's easy to become paranoid, reflecting on the various disasters that might befall me or my family. But those disasters will come whether I expect them or not. Stewing about them won't prevent them, and worrying about them won't make them less difficult to face when they get here.

The most important thing that going through something like this prepares you for is to have compassion for others in their times of need. I have learned so much about what my neighbors and friends have suffered as they have reached out to me in sympathy. Marilee lost her son a few years ago and is now a chaplain, assisting others as they process the trauma of sickness and death. Eric lost his father very suddenly and struggled to know how to believe that the hero of his boyhood would no longer be there to teach and guide him. Melinda's husband fell off a ladder and was paralyzed from the neck down, catapulting them both into early retirement and changing the dynamic of their marriage forever. Natalie got incredibly sick and had to be on bed rest for months while trying to care for her small children. Loren and Lori lost their husbands. Susan was in a terrible car accident. Katrina struggled with chronic illness and infertility. Nikki has crippling attacks of vertigo that doctors are unable to treat.

As these people reach out to me, I can feel so clearly how their trials have prepared them to help me. They have eyes that see and hearts that understand. They know how to mourn with those who mourn and comfort those who stand in need of comfort (see Mosiah 18:9). I never feel like they are trying to upstage me or belittle me or fix me. Like the Savior Himself, they are people "of sorrows and acquainted with grief" (Isaiah 53:4), and they have been prepared, as He was, to succor others because of the things they have suffered.

This is the greatest work that there is: ministering to others when the weight of this life becomes too much for them to bear alone. Of all the things that Jesus taught us during His life, this is the thing that stands out the most. Serve. Care for each other. Care about each other. Make sure no one in the sphere of your influence walks alone through the valley.

No matter what else happens to me for the rest of my life, whether or not this is the last great trial that I face, this is the work that losing my son qualifies me for in a new and unique way. As I seek and expect miracles, I will need to start seeking and expecting to find opportunities to put this preparation to use. I pray that my eyes will be open to see who needs me and that my feet will not be weary in walking alongside those who tread the dark paths of grief and sorrow for a time. The sun seems to find us much more quickly when we don't have to walk alone.

7
The Miracle of Confession

The really unfair part about your world completely falling apart is that you aren't allowed to fall apart with it.

The Monday that Dallin fell was a day of holding it together. From the moment we got the call, our lives became one endless stream of tasks that required us to be mentally and emotionally intact. We had to get our other kids from school, explain to them what was going on, and find someone to take care of them. We had to drive to the hospital without crashing. We had to listen to the doctors and try to ask them intelligible questions. We had to comfort, and try to appear to be comforted by, all the relatives and friends who came to be with us at the hospital. We had to respond to the barrage of text messages and phone calls coming in as people tried to figure out what was going on and how they could help. It was one big gut-wrenching marathon of holding it together.

As the day wore on, I began to get more and more worried about my husband. He suffers from one of the signature military disabilities: chronic anxiety and depression coupled with a crippling inability to talk about those feelings. The reasons behind these symptoms are plentiful and complex, but that is a topic for a different book, preferably one written by an expert in the field. For my purposes, it is enough to say that the more Tim continued to appear to be okay, the more I worried that irreparable damage was occurring in his heart and mind.

He needed a release, and it wasn't clear to me whether he would get one before he reached a critical breaking point.

* * *

There is a principle taught in Christianity that has gotten a bad reputation in recent years because it is so often misunderstood or abused. This is the principle of confession. The scriptures are full of it.

- Leviticus 5:5— "And it shall be, when he shall be guilty in one of these things, that he shall confess that he hath sinned in that thing."
- Joshua 7:19—"And Joshua said unto Achan, My son, give, I pray thee, glory to the Lord God of Israel, and make confession unto him; and tell me now what thou hast done; hide it not from me."
- Mosiah 26:29—"And if he confess his sins before thee and me, and repenteth in the sincerity of his heart, him shall ye forgive, and I will forgive him also."
- Doctrine and Covenants 61:2—"I, the Lord, forgive sins, and am merciful unto those who confess their sins with humble hearts."

Prophets are primarily concerned with the salvation of our souls, so they really lean into the necessity of confessing our sins in order to receive forgiveness. Most scriptures, sermons, or guidelines on the subject of confession will be related to forgiveness of sins and, directly from there, the salvation of the soul. Too often, people perceive this doctrine as being manipulative or shame-inducing, mostly because corrupt individuals never seem to run out of ways to use it as a tool for wickedness.

Many see confession as simply one more way for the patriarchal leadership of a religion to force members to kowtow to their authority. Unfortunately, there are plenty of real-life examples, both modern and ancient, of corrupt leaders inside and outside Christianity doing exactly that. On the other hand, the rich, powerful, and manipulative have often used confession as a way to fake their own repentance or even keep their sins hidden. They insist that those they have hurt *must* forgive them because, after all, they have confessed to the proper authority. No one is allowed to mention their transgressions or hold them accountable for their bad behavior. In their view, they have ticked the box of confession and that ought to be enough for everyone. In recent years, it has become fashionable for politicians and other prominent figures to offer public apologies, many of which are just insincere confessions. It is a marketing tool meant to placate the masses without requiring any change of feeling or behavior on the part of the sinner. The list goes on and on.

Anyone who has undergone true repentance knows that these abuses are an abomination—counterfeits of what confession really means and what it's really for. Confession is meant to bring about godly sorrow that lifts your eyes to the Lord and gives you hope that you can be better through His grace. And it is meant to help you recognize the people you have hurt and your duty to make every effort at restitution.[6] It helps us define what is problematic in our behavior and gain greater insight into our hearts and motivations. Confession requires humility, a broken heart and a contrite spirit, and a recognition that we can't do this alone. But it is also uplifting, healing, brave, honest, and kind. As with Alma the Younger, confession lifts the weight of hell from our souls and gives us new motivation and direction (see Mosiah 27; Alma 36).

As I have passed through certain trials and attempted to follow President Nelson's counsel to "hear Him,"[7] I have come to understand that the doctrine of confession has a wider scope than just confession of my sins. It's a good place to start, for sure, and most of us need to get good at confessing our sins in order to build a solid relationship with Jesus. But most days, I find myself needing to confess other things: my anger, my disappointment, my exhaustion, my gratitude, my joy, my confusion, my fear.

We were sent to this earth to gain experience, and experience means emotion. It's not a sin to feel things. I don't even think it's a sin to feel hatred or despair or greed. We have to experience the "negative" along with the positive. But the trick of mortality is learning to feel the emotions that come to us without feeding them so that they consume

---

6. See James A. Cullimore, "Confession and Forsaking: Elements of Genuine Repentance," *Ensign*, Nov. 1971, 85–87.

7. Russell M. Nelson, "Hear Him," *Ensign* or *Liahona*, May 2020, 88.

us. And that is where confession will help us. When we confess our feelings to God, He magnifies the ones that bring us closer to Him and gives us a measure of relief from the ones that push us away from Him.[8] As with confession of sins, confession of feelings helps us pinpoint what exactly is going on in our hearts so we can understand what we're going through and how God can help us with it. It requires us to be honest, vulnerable, and humble and to recognize that we could really use some help because emotions are heavy and we are weak. Jesus, who "hath borne our griefs, and carried our sorrows" (Isaiah 53:4), is strong and will help us bear them again.

I can't count the number of times when just telling the Lord (out loud) that I was angry gave me the space I needed to pass through the anger and find the peace on the other side. When we share our emotional burdens with the Lord through confession, we yoke with Him. And we find that "[his] yoke is easy and [his] burden is light" (Matthew 11:30). The weight of hell is lifted from our souls.

Is there any doubt that grief is among the weightiest of emotions?

Is there any hell on earth more palpable than walking through the valley of the shadow of death alone?

If we are to survive our grief, we must confess it.

* * *

When the hospital staff called to let me know that a Ronald McDonald House bedroom had been reserved for Tim and me that Monday night, I was grateful beyond words. It was very late when we were finally able to lie down, but the minute we did, all of my husband's carefully controlled grief came spilling out of him. He completely fell apart. And I was so relieved.

"I can't hold it together. I can't be strong," he said.

"Fall apart. Don't worry about it. Just hold on to me. Stay with me."

We have been married for seventeen years, and I can't remember ever seeing Tim really cry. He got misty a few times at church events and significant milestones with our children. He was on the verge of tears when he spoke at his father's funeral. He gets a little choked up

---

8. See David A. Bednar, "Bear Up Their Burdens with Ease," *Ensign* or *Liahona*, May 2014, 87–90.

during war movies. But that night in the hospital, the walls that had so effectively dammed his more vulnerable feelings finally came down. His body shook, and he whimpered like a wounded animal. It was awkward and unfamiliar for him after so many years, and I worried he would pull back before it all came out. But he didn't. He kept the floodgates open until his confession was complete, and it was a miracle.

I held him tight, and we cried the tears of the brokenhearted. We didn't feel less sad when we were through. But we were able to sleep for a little while.

When Tim confessed his grief and weakness, he yoked himself to me and we yoked ourselves to Jesus. And together we made it through the night. We found what peace there was to be had. And it was enough.

8
The Miracle of Faith

When Tim and I went to bed on Monday, we made a pact that we wouldn't make any concrete decisions about what to do until the morning. We would give it the night.

Well, I forgot to turn off my regular alarm on my phone, so at 5:30 a.m., it shook me out of my sleep. With the volume on my ringer turned down, it hadn't been enough to wake Tim up, so I quickly grabbed my shoes and slipped out of the room and into the common area. There, tying up my laces, I had to confront a horrible reality.

The night was over.

It was morning.

Today we would have to make decisions.

I hadn't thought to grab a toothbrush when I left the house the day before, so I swigged some water and headed off to see Dallin. He wouldn't care what my breath smelled like, and I was impatient to see him.

It's difficult to describe what I felt sitting next to my unconscious son, listening to the machines push air into and out of his lungs, knowing in my soul that I was out of time. As a person who is both educated and religious, there are two types of faith that pull on me in times of crisis, and they always seem to be in competition with each other.

The first is that childlike faith you have that nothing is impossible—like faith in the Jesus who walked on water, who healed the ten lepers, and who raised Lazarus from the dead. This type of faith tells you to ignore the data, to disregard what conventional science tells you, to charge forward recklessly, hoping, *knowing* even, that Jesus will make everything okay. He will grant your heart's desire if only you believe hard enough. I subscribe to that kind of faith. I believe that Moses parted the Red Sea, I believe that the daughter of Jairus came back to life after being declared dead, and I believe that Lehi and Nephi were encircled about with fire and that it burned them not (see Exodus 14; Mark 5; Helaman 5). I believe it all, and I always try to make room for that kind of faith when disaster strikes. After all, I wouldn't want to keep God from working a miracle for me by not believing He will.

The second kind of faith is the faith of the realist: the logical mind. The faith that tells me to look at the evidence, accept the inevitable, and believe that God will give me the strength to endure it. A different kind of miracle—much less flashy but very utilitarian. I subscribe to this kind of faith as well. It has seen me through many years and countless trials.

Sitting there with Dallin that morning, I tried to make room for both types of faith. It was hard. I found myself doing something that I don't do often, mostly because when people do it in scripture stories, it does not go well for them. I asked for a sign.

I told God that I believed—I *knew* that He could raise Dallin from the dead if He willed it. I told Him I didn't want to tell the doctors to let Dallin die if God intended to save him in some miraculous fashion. Moreover, Dallin's heart was still beating. How could I be the one to make it stop? If I told the doctors to turn off the machines, I would be the one who killed him. It would be *my* decision to stop his heart and end his life. How could I do that without a sign? How could I say the words without an angel or a vision or the voice of God instructing me to do it?

"I need a sign," I pleaded. "I can't say those words without a sign."

I cried some more. There's no end of crying when your child is dying. And I started singing. I've always sung to the kids to comfort them, just like my mom and dad did for me. My children know my voice from inside the womb, before they even knew who I was or how completely they were already relying on me. I sing them songs from musicals, old spirituals from my choir days, and church songs and folk songs, mixed in with some more classic lullabies. I sang Dallin some of our favorites, and a memory began to form in my mind.

When Dallin was born, there was a moment during labor when I sensed that he was afraid. It's hard to describe how I knew it. It was just one of those times when spiritual communication comes strong and fast, and you're absolutely sure. Dallin was afraid. He had been warm and comfortable for nine months as he grew inside of me, and he didn't like what was happening to him. All the squeezing and the pushing and the noises and the lights—he hated every bit of it. It was the first time I had really looked at the labor and delivery process from the perspective of the baby, and I realized it must be a pretty harrowing experience. So I tried to reach out to his spirit and reassure him.

"Don't be afraid. I know this is hard, but it will be over soon, and I will be here when you get through it to love you and hold you and help you forget that you were ever afraid."

On that Tuesday morning, sitting alone with my boy in the very early hours of the morning—in a room made sacred by my prayers, my tears, and my song—the spiritual communication came fast and strong, and once again I was sure. This was the day we had to let him go. And in that moment, it was as if he was saying my own words back to me.

"Don't be afraid, Mom. I know this is hard, but it will be over soon, and I will be here when you get through it to love you and hold you."

I had my sign. And as sure as I know anything, I know that though Dallin was sad to leave us, this time he wasn't afraid.

A little over a month after Dallin died, I gave a lesson to the twelve- and thirteen-year-old girls at my church about the daughter of Jairus who was raised from the dead. In that story, Jairus comes to Jesus in the city and asks him to come to his home and heal his daughter who is "at the point of death" (Mark 5:23). Jesus agrees. It takes them time to make their way through the crowd, though, and when they finally reach Jairus's house, a servant meets them outside the door and informs them that the daughter has died. Now, having sat in a hospital room holding the hand of my own child who was "at the point of death," I can imagine exactly what this father felt in that moment. But I can also imagine exactly how Jesus must have grabbed Jairus by the arm, gripping him tightly and looking straight in his eyes as He said the words that He says to all of us in our moments of greatest danger and deepest despair.

"Be not afraid, only believe" (Mark 5:36).

I told those girls, and I will say it here: I would have given anything for Jesus to raise my son from the dead like He did for Jairus's little girl. There's no price I wouldn't have paid, no distance I wouldn't have traveled, no sacrifice I wouldn't have offered. But I know that in the end, because of Jesus, the outcome for Dallin is the same as it was for her. That story is our promise that death is not the end of life. I will see Dallin again.

Jesus has power over death, so just as Dallin was not afraid to leave, so I was not afraid to let him go. I was heartbroken, weary, sick with disappointment, and still not convinced that all this wasn't some horrible dream. But I was not afraid.

Between the sobs that racked my whole body, I squeezed Dallin's hand and promised him that if he would hold on for one more day so that the people who love him could come and say goodbye, then I would let him go at the end of it.

9
The Miracle of Science

Before I went to see Tim that morning, I had a quick chat with the doctor.

Sometime on Monday, they had hooked Dallin up to an EEG, which basically measures brain activity. On Tuesday morning, the EEG was disconnected. The night shift doctor was still on duty, so I asked him why. I knew I would need to have my facts straight about Dallin's condition when I talked to Tim about what needed to be done.

The doctor said that the EEG readings had been consistent throughout the night, and nothing more could be learned from them. Armed with a few hours of sleep and a new resolve, I asked him to explain to me very clearly exactly what those readings were and what they meant. He told me that Dallin's brain had alternated between periods of flatlining and series of random electric bursts. There was no organized brain activity—no possibility of independent function.

Now, if I'm being honest with myself, I'm pretty sure the daytime doctor had given me the same information the day before at the end of his shift. I had flat-out asked him whether, in his professional opinion, there was any chance that Dallin would get better. He had said no. But I hadn't been in a correct mental state to ask the follow-up questions I needed to fully comprehend what he was telling me. After all, "get better" can mean so many different things.

But this time I was ready to understand what I was hearing, clarify those points that were still a little murky, and know what I needed to do. I had already promised Dallin we would let him go by the end of the day, but now I could go to my husband with more than just a feeling. I had data. We could be sure.

Some people will tell you that faith and science are incompatible—that they are so fundamentally contradictory that it is impossible for them to coexist in the same mind. I haven't found that to be true. Everything I learn about God's plan for His children shows me that the universe is much bigger than I could ever imagine. What I understand is such a tiny part of what is, and God constantly encourages us to seek out more, to expand our minds and widen our view. The systematic pursuit of truth is a uniquely scientific principle, one that is in complete harmony with faith.

Science confirms truth through physical senses. Revelation confirms truth through spiritual senses. They are both miracles—gifts from a loving Heavenly Father who wants us to receive all that He has (Doctrine and Covenants 84:38). These truths will not come into conflict as long as we are patient, humble, and discerning. The one will confirm the other, bringing stability and longevity to the fundamental truths that make up the firm foundation of our belief system. As beings of both flesh and spirit, we are privileged to access truth through the full array of our senses, thus gaining a broader, more profound understanding of how the universe functions. We shouldn't rely only on our spiritual senses, just as we shouldn't rely only on our sense of touch if we are also receiving information through our sense of smell. Cutting ourselves off from science shrinks our perspective and makes us small-minded, fragile, and more vulnerable to attacks on our faith. I think this is especially true in times of crisis and difficult decisions.

The Lord has promised to confirm the truth to us "in the mouth of two or three witnesses" (2 Corinthians 13:1), and when life and death hang in the balance, we need all the witnesses we can get. Science may seem cold and calculating in times when our heart is breaking, but that's one of the things that makes it such a miracle. Science can't be fooled into being something it's not because we're sad about the way things are turning out. Sometimes we need a break from so emotionally experiencing the tragedy so that we can see what's going on more clearly. For me, on that Tuesday morning when time had run out and we had to decide the fate of our son, the miracle of science took some of the awful weight of responsibility from my shoulders. We didn't have to act on my feelings alone. The data showed that, in spite of the doctors' miraculous ability to force his heart to keep pumping and push air into and out of his lungs, Dallin's body was damaged beyond repair. Even with the machines, he would eventually die. Based on this data, our decision became not so much whether or not we would keep him alive but how long we would allow him to suffer. How long would we chain Dallin's spirit to a body that had already ceased to live?

I'm grateful for the interventions that kept Dallin's heart beating. They gave us time, and time with the ones we love is precious. The miracle of science kept his body going long enough for us to say goodbye.

And I'm grateful for the second witness I received from medical experts wielding cold, hard facts that confirmed the truth I had received earlier through spiritual channels. The miracle of science helped us accept that it was time to let Dallin go.

10

The Miracle of Revelation

My conversation with Tim didn't take long. He had read the signs as well as I had, and the final EEG reports confirmed to him as they had to me that our son's body didn't really belong to him anymore. So we started making phone calls.

Dallin had made a lot of friends in his short eight years, even in the year and a half that he lived in the Tooele Valley. So we only invited close family to come to the hospital to say goodbye. But even that list was long. We knew it would be another grueling day, and we would have to give my parents time to fly in from California before it would be over.

Looking back, I wish I had had a butler of sorts to man the waiting room and escort people in and out of Dallin's room, ensuring each party got equal time and that their needs were attended to during their stay. That way I could have just stayed with Dallin as long as I wanted and retreated to a dark corner to close my eyes when it was too much. But hospital waiting room butler isn't a job in the service industry yet, as far as I know, so the task fell to us. And though everyone who came cared about us deeply and wanted to lift and support us, the day grew more and more difficult as the hours wore on.

On the other hand, there was also something very sacred about the time we spent in the hospital that day, hugging and crying and talking and even laughing. Revelation comes easily around a deathbed, when the veil between our world and the spirit world is stretched to its paper-thin limits, when the spirit of a child hovers on the precipice of eternity. It's easy to sink under the weight of the millstone of regrets chained around your mind, but it's just as easy to snatch shards of insight and glorious truth, sharp and strong enough to break those chains and set you free.

The regrets that swarmed Tim and me were mostly of the "nevermore" variety. They were realizations that came to us in spurts and waves. Tim would never get to take Dallin on a father-son campout. Dallin would never get to sleep in the bedroom we were getting finished for him in the basement. (He had spent almost all his money on posters and knickknacks to decorate it.) I would never get to teach him to play piano or how to sing harmonies with me and the girls. He would never get to go to the junior high school that is being built around the corner from our house. We would never look over and see him sitting on the pews with his friends, waiting to pass the sacrament in church. He wouldn't even get to play in the soccer tournament just a couple of weeks away that he had been looking forward to for months. All the things we had been planning on and looking forward to had changed from joyful expectations to full stop impossibilities, darts in our open wounds to poison our broken hearts.

The revelation that came to me in the temple of our affliction was that those nevermores were, in fact, a lie. One of the great truths of the Restoration is that the afterlife is not a place of stagnation. It's not even a place of relaxation. There are things to learn, progress to be made, and work to be done.[9] The prophets teach us that we don't leave this world to go sit on a cloud; we leave so we can move forward with life—so that we can live our best life actually. What the Spirit reminded me that day is that Dallin isn't really missing anything. He's not having the exact same experiences he would have had if he'd stayed with us, but he's not missing out either. He's living his absolute best life, learning and helping people and making friends. One day soon he'll have important work to do, and he's going to be awesome at it. All of his

---

9. See Brent L. Top, "What Is This Thing That Men Call Death? Latter-day Saint Teachings About the Spirit World" (Brigham Young University devotional, Aug. 18, 2020), speeches.byu.edu.

smarts, his talents, his humor, his outgoing nature—they are making him unstoppable. And the things I got to teach him here on earth have prepared him for the life he's living now on the other side of the veil. He'll still be a part of our lives, involved in our problems, interested in our progress, and present at our special events. But he's got his own life now, and he's living it.

Almost instantaneously, this revelation stripped me of any sense of regret. There's sadness still—buckets of it. There's a deep sense of bittersweetness every time I wonder what we'll do with the room that was supposed to be his when it's finished. I don't know that I'll ever watch a soccer game without feeling a deep ache of longing for my Dallin. But no regret.

The parable that came to my mind that Tuesday was of a mother who dreams her son will be a doctor. She imagines the schools he'll attend and the honors he'll win there. She picks out a dress to wear to his graduation and plans out how best to tastefully brag to her friends and relatives about "my son, the doctor." All her plans for the future are woven into the expectation that he will fulfill her fondest dreams.

But as her son grows older, he realizes he wants to be something else—something unconventional that takes him far from home. He pursues that career with passion and determination. He tries to tell his mother how important his work is, how happy it makes him, but all she can do is sigh with regret.

"If only you could have been a doctor," she laments, "then we could have been so happy."

This poor son. No matter how much success he achieves, no matter how deep his conviction that he is making the right choice, he will never have a fullness of joy in the life he chooses for himself. Because he will always carry the weight of his mother's disappointment.

I realized that day and I say it again to myself now: I don't want to be that mother. I don't want my son's joy to be diminished because I'm consumed with disappointment that he didn't live the life I dreamed he would. I want him to live his life on his own terms and to know that he has my full support. He didn't leave us. He wasn't taken from us, not really. He was offered a scholarship at a prestigious boarding school, and he took it. After that, he'll have an exciting overseas job opportunity that he'll gladly accept. Obviously, it all happened much sooner than I was ready for, and I miss him terribly. He'll see the tear stains on the letters I send him and hear the quaver in my voice when I say goodbye at the end of our very spotty cell phone calls. But I promise not to resent him or the Lord because his life took a different direction than the one I planned on. He'll always know that I'm immeasurably proud of him and everything he's accomplishing while he's away. And I'm so excited for him to tell me all about it when I see him again. I almost can't wait.

Interestingly, not every heart will resonate with the truth I came to know that day. My heart finds great comfort in knowing Dallin's life is going on quite normally without me. It helps me let go of the "nevermores" and not drown myself in a quagmire of "might have beens." But others yearn for a message of restitution—a reassurance that all the experiences they missed having with their child will be restored to them through the power of the Atonement. They want to know that the baby they once held in their arms will belong to them to nurture and to raise in the Millennium.[10] I've had quotes and anecdotes about this particular doctrine spouted at me by all kinds of people, and to be honest, it all leaves me a little cold. It's certainly not what I needed to hear on the day I had to say goodbye to my son.

The miraculous thing about revelation is that it's tailored to your needs. Although revelation is always true when it comes from God, not every person is comforted by every truth. A full inventory of the details of eternity will never be made available to us in this life. I imagine we couldn't understand it if it were. Our minds are just too mired in this temporal world of timelines and finite possibilities. So the Father counsels each of us to find our own holy places in which to seek our own personal revelation. There are many truths available to the children of God, and only our Father understands which of these truths will be comforting and sustaining to us in our times of trial.

The miracle of revelation isn't necessarily the thing that is revealed. The miracle is that each of us can have the thing we need revealed to us in the time that we need it. Seeking miracles means striving to live that higher law that will bring us into closer, constant contact with the

10. See *Teachings of Presidents of the Church: Joseph F. Smith* (1998), 128–135.

Holy Ghost so that revelation can flow to us more effortlessly and we can understand it when it comes.[11]

11. See Richard G. Scott, "Truth" (Brigham Young University devotional, June 13, 1978), speeches.byu.edu.

11
The Miracle of Music

As the hours stretched out and the day wound down, I began to get anxious. Many people had come and gone, but others had stayed, determined to be with us until the end.

My sister brought my kids to the hospital after an early dinner. I know other families would have wanted to be all together for the whole day, and there's nothing wrong with a family making that decision. But for us, I felt like a hospital would be a horrible place for a kid to spend so many hours with so little to do except think about the fact that their brother is dying. When my girls arrived—Abigail, Macaylie, and Margaret—a woman from the hospital's child services team came and helped us make canvases with their handprints next to Dallin's handprint. Then we made one with all of our handprints around the edges of the canvas, with Dallin's in the middle. I was the one to take Dallin's little hand and place it where we wanted it on the canvas. It was more difficult than I thought it would be, almost as if I still expected him to help me out by lifting his arm a bit or spreading his fingers the way he automatically would have done if he were conscious. It was such a sweet service for the hospital to provide us, and we will treasure those mementos for the rest of our lives.

In the early evening, my parents finally arrived from California with my sister who lives with them. She has an autoimmune disease and, because of her health issues, has cultivated a very special relationship with all of her nieces and nephews. I sent them in to sit with Dallin while we finished our projects. Then Abigail, Macaylie, Margaret, Tim and I went in to join them. It was time to say goodbye.

It's hard to know what to say to someone who's dying who is such an integral part of your life. What do you want them to know? What do you think they would want to hear? Once you start, how can you just be finished, knowing that being finished means never seeing them alive again? It's impossible, yet we have to do it. The closure that comes with goodbye is important to our fragile human psyches, and we should take it whenever we can get it.

Luckily for my family, we have music. There is something about music that opens up your heart and lets you communicate more freely. When you sing a song to someone you love, you share an experience that transcends words. All your feelings, all your hopes, all your secret thoughts—they somehow get woven into the melody and stitched into the fabric of the lyrics. Your loved one gets the message, and you receive it right back. It's a miracle.

Just as my kids have known my voice since before they were born, I have known my parents' voices, especially my dad's. My father is a slender guy—I've outweighed him most of my adult life—so it's always a bit of a surprise for people who don't know him when he sings in his rich, resonant, deep bass. His voice is somehow bigger than he is. It fills a room, and I learned most of what I know about expressiveness and musical sensitivity from listening to him practice at home and perform at church. "The Trumpet Shall Sound" from Handel's *Messiah* is his signature song, along with a lovely piece called "Little Lamb," whose words are a famous poem by William Blake.

> Little Lamb, who made thee?
> Dost thou know who made thee?
> Gave thee life and bid thee feed
> By the stream and o'er the mead? [...]
> Little Lamb, I'll tell thee!
> He is called by thy name,
> For He calls Himself a Lamb;
> He is meek and He is mild,
> He became a little child:
> I a child and thou a lamb,

We are called by His name.[12]

We've passed photocopies of that song around my family for years because we just can't seem to find a legal copy of it, and it's too beautiful to stop singing. Of all the things I've sung in my life, "Little Lamb" is the most intimidating because I know I'll never sing it well enough to live up to the memory I have of my dad singing it. In my mind, his performances are perfect and shiny, flawlessly executed in every way. I know that memory is romanticized and unrealistic, but I'm grateful for it, especially now. The love of the Savior that music planted in my young heart was real, and on that day it was the thing I needed most.

We didn't sing my dad's signature songs that evening in the hospital. Showy, demanding performance pieces are not meant for a deathbed, even if they're beautiful. But those songs were in my heart, especially with my mom and dad there helping me sing Dallin his last lullabies. My child, knit to Jesus by name and faith, was being called home to the One who knows and loves him best. The life that was given was about to be taken away, not by a cold, formless force of justice but by the Lamb of God—someone we know, someone like us, someone who knows what it's like to comfort His mother because her Son is dying before she was ready. And yet that's not the end of the story.

The trumpet shall sound,
And the dead shall be raised,
Be raised incorruptible.[13]

The promise of a triumphant Resurrection and a glorious reunion with all the Saints of God reverberated in my soul that day. I can't say that it helped me feel any better necessarily. Knowing things will get better doesn't always help you feel better about things being awful in the moment. But it does help in a different way. Knowing that our separation and the pain that goes with it have an expiration date helped me be patient in bearing it. It still helps.

---

12. "The Lamb Summary & Analysis by William Blake," LitCharts, accessed Jan. 6, 2024, https://www.litcharts.com/poetry/william-blake/the-lamb.

13. "The Trumpet Shall Sound," Musixmatch, accessed Jan. 6, 2024, https://www.musixmatch.com/lyrics/George-Frideric-Handel-EvandroOlivah/The-Trumpet-Shall-Sound.

The song we sang for Dallin was one that the kids learned at church called "Gethsemane." It's all about Jesus's experience in the Garden of Gethsemane—how brave He was to go in, how strong He was to stay, and how much we love Him for the sacrifice He made for us there.

> Gethsemane. Jesus loves me,
> So He went willingly to Gethsemane.
> The hardest thing that ever was done,
> The greatest pain that ever was known,
> The biggest battle that ever was won—
> This was done by Jesus!
> The fight was won by Jesus![14]

Dallin sang that song with us for Tim's biological dad, Greg, when he was in hospice care, only months away from dying. It's a song that brings the Holy Ghost into a room effortlessly, and we all needed the Comforter that day. We sang to comfort each other and Dallin. We sang to reaffirm our love for him and for each other. We sang to declare our faith in Jesus and to remind ourselves that this was a temporary goodbye. We sang to mourn. We sang to rejoice. We sang to fill the darkness with light. There was no other way to say what we needed to say.

---

14. Melanie Hoffman, "Gethsemane," *Friend*, Mar. 2018, 28–29.

12
The Miracle of Goodbye

After we sang and everyone gave Dallin a kiss goodbye, we sent everyone away except for Tim and me. Despite the sweet sadness we felt being all together as a family, my anxiety was increasing. I had promised Dallin he could go if he stayed for the day. He had patiently waited, the evening had come, and I didn't want him to feel like I was dragging my feet about keeping my promise to him.

We told the doctors we were ready, and they began to get everything arranged. The day shift nurse who had taken care of Dallin Monday and Tuesday stayed to help the night shift nurse with everything. There were machines to be adjusted, tubes to be disconnected, furniture to be rearranged, and final explanations to be made. Finally, they were ready.

Tim had asked if he could be the one to hold Dallin at the end, so we sat him in the most comfortable chair we could find, one that would be easy on his aching back, and I sat on a chair next to him. The doctors transferred Dallin from the bed to Tim's lap. He'd gotten so tall that most of his legs were in my lap. Normally he looked so small next to his teenage sisters, but at that moment all I could think was how big he'd gotten. I used to snuggle him so easily in my lap in one little bundle, and here he was, sprawled over the both of us, wrapped in a blanket that Child Services had gifted us. My little man, so big and tall.

We held him as the doctor removed the breathing tube and stopped the blood pressure medication. Then they left the room to give us some privacy. Dallin's body took some gasping breaths the way bodies do when they get taken off machines and the automatic fail-safes kick in and make one last-ditch effort to save the body. But it was much less violent than I have heard stories of it being for other people.

We sang Dallin "You Wonderful You," which is an old song from a Judy Garland musical called *Summer Stock*. It was the one I sang to him most often at bedtime. Tim had sung it to him the night just before the accident. Dallin had been having trouble falling asleep and went in to see Tim who was sitting in the family room watching a movie. Tim is always the better one to go to at night because he's less likely to get mad than me. Dallin crawled into Tim's lap and Tim sang him this song. There's a part where the words say:

> Remember finders keepers, losers weepers
> And because it's true, you're mine now,
> You wonderful you.[15]

Tim changed the words a little bit.

> Remember finders keepers, losers weepers
> And because it's true, you're my son,
> You wonderful you.

We sang it that way. I think I'll always sing it that way in my heart from now on. It was such a gift to have such a sweet moment so fresh in our minds to remind us of how completely and truly we belong to each other despite this temporary, premature goodbye.

There was nothing to say or do—just wait and feel the sadness wash over us.

Poor Tim turned to me and said through tears, "How can this be?"

We cried a little longer and I sang "For Good" from the musical *Wicked*. It's another song I think I'll always secretly be singing to Dallin, no matter where or when or to whom I'm actually singing it.

Tim turned to me again and said, "Thank you for letting me hold him."

---

15. Gene Kelly, "You Wonderful You," track 10 on *'S Wonderful,* Rhino, 1996, compact disc. Lyrics found at https://genius.com/Gene-kelly-you-wonderful-you-lyrics.

I said, "I carried him in; you carry him out."

Tim broke down even more and sobbed, "We shouldn't have to."

We shouldn't have to. It's not right. This isn't the way it's supposed to be. Just a split second to change the course of events and everything would be different. We could be home putting him to bed instead of here watching him die. It isn't fair. We shouldn't have to.

But it was happening. It's not right, but it's real. And we have to survive it.

Only with Jesus.

It was probably only about ten minutes before Dallin's body was completely still.

The doctor came in and very gently said, "You've probably noticed that Dallin isn't breathing anymore." He listened for a full two minutes for a heartbeat with his stethoscope and then said, "I'm very sorry to tell you that Dallin has died."

How do you hear those words that are so unfair? How do you give that news to parents who aren't ready, no matter how much preparation they've had? How do we survive it? How do people go through this who don't have the gospel—who don't have the gift of the Holy Ghost right with them the whole time? I can't imagine it. I don't want to live in a world where I have to face a single day without that gift. It's too heavy. It's too much.

The nurse moved Dallin's body back to the bed. Already he didn't look like himself anymore. In a matter of moments, he had gone from being my son to being just the body of my son—the glove without the hand.[16] I was glad he had left so quickly. He'd been saying goodbye to people all day long, and he slipped eagerly and quietly out of mortality as soon as he was able. It was easier to feel the closure of our last goodbye knowing that he was already on his way. I repositioned his blanket so that his body was fully covered.

I thanked the doctor and the nurses for taking such good care of our son, and we left the PICU for the last time.

---

16. See Boyd K. Packer, "Behold Your Little Ones," *Ensign*, May 1973, 51–54.

13
The Miracles That Come After

Walking back down the hall toward the private waiting room that had been our base of operations for the past two days, I felt overwhelmed by how tired I was. I slipped past our friends and sank down next to my sisters.

"I want to go home" was all I could say.

"Let's make that happen."

They cleaned up the room, gathered the trash and the leftover snacks, and hustled the girls out as fast as they would be hustled. They did their best, bless them, but Tim and I were still the last ones out.

I drove us home. There wasn't much to say.

When we pulled up to our house, there were construction paper hearts on the garage and yellow ribbons tied around the many trees in our front yard as well as the two pillars that frame our front door. I'm not sure why, but I found those ribbons immensely comforting.

These were the first of many miraculous gestures from friends, family, and our community that lifted us up over the following days and weeks. I'll name just a few.

Dallin's elementary school, whose students and faculty had been so profoundly affected by our tragedy, made us a banner and cards expressing their love. They're still hanging in my living room. Dallin's class bought a soccer ball and had all of his classmates sign it. The PTA raised funds and made T-shirts for all the kids in the school as well as our family that say "Celebrando Dallin." (It's a Portuguese immersion school.) On the day they wore the shirts, they gathered all the students and faculty and took a picture, then printed a copy on a large canvas that we displayed at the funeral. For the rest of the school year, whenever I went to the school to drop something off or help out with an event, at least one kid would be wearing their shirt. I love to see that they remember him. Dallin's teachers set up a basket at the back of the classroom where the kids could leave little notes or gifts for Dallin whenever they found something that reminded them of him or just felt lonely without him. I had substitute taught those kids a number of times, and knowing they had such a sensitive therapeutic tool so close by helped me not to worry about them so much.

One woman in particular felt so moved when she heard about Dallin's accident that she began collecting donations from people and businesses all around the community. She was the one behind the yellow ribbons. As I gradually ventured farther from the house over the next few days, I realized those ribbons were everywhere—at every nearby school, on the trees along the main road by our house, in random people's front yards. They stayed for over a month before they began falling down and becoming a bit of a litter problem, and I missed them after they were removed.

Dallin's soccer team put together a care package that they delivered right before they all left to play in their big tournament. At their games, they displayed a banner with Dallin's picture and wore arm bands with his number on them. The boys told their parents and coaches that they would play extra hard for Dallin.

Our wonderful friend of many years set up a GoFundMe page for us, which hundreds of people donated to, many of whom we don't know. She also volunteered to speak to the many reporters who wanted to do stories about Dallin, and she did a great job. It was an incredible way to lift those burdens from us in our time of immediate crisis.

Our church and neighborhood friends gathered together one night and made luminaries, which are white paper bags you decorate and then put tea lights in. Each family made two: one for our home and one for theirs. For as many days as the snow would hold off, dozens of flickering paper lanterns lined our porch and sidewalk. They shone from the porches of our neighbors, reminding us of all the love and support we were surrounded by—reminding us of the light of Christ that will guide our footsteps as we make our way forward through the darkness of the valley.

A neighbor I had never met before came by and told me about her child who had died, and she gave me a book she had written about the things that had helped her get through that time.

The local Denny's restaurant put words of support and love for Dallin (and another local boy who had died) on their large message board.

A member of our community made beautiful black-and-white pencil drawings of Dallin based on his last school picture and framed them for us. The photography company that did the last picture day at Dallin's school made free prints of his school pictures for us in a variety of sizes. An anonymous donor had a special quilt made for us with this same picture printed on it, which was displayed at the funeral.

People from church and the neighborhood brought food for my family every night for over a month, and I'm sure they would still be bringing it if I asked them. One friend from church offered to provide flowers for the funeral for free. Another provided photography services. Another made Christmas ornaments for my immediate family members out of small prints of Dallin's handprint that Child Services had provided us with. The youth ages 12–18 showed up in droves at church on the day of the funeral to clean the building for us. Our bishop and his wife came over many, many times to check in on us and make sure we were being taken care of.

Tim's family has been there for us. Tons of them came to the funeral and burial to show their love and support. His immediate family reached out in countless ways and are still careful to check in with us to make sure we're okay.

And then, of course, there are my sisters. All five of them, as well as my mother, came and stayed with me for as long as their families could spare them. It's really impossible to describe how big of a support they were to me. They distracted and entertained my daughters so I could disappear into my room whenever I needed to. I think one of the big reasons my girls have been able to process their feelings so well is that they weren't left alone to stew and worry in those first difficult days. There were people they trusted all around them to cuddle with, laugh with, play with, and (occasionally) be still with. My sisters ran every errand, wrote every thank you card, washed every dish, vacuumed every rug, cleaned every bathroom. When we came home from the funeral with vases full of flowers, they pulled out the stepladder and put them on top of my kitchen cabinets. They changed a cluttered mess into a beautiful garden I could wake up to every morning for as long as it lasted. They sat with me when I wanted company, retreated when I wanted solitude, and basically filled the empty corners of our home so the transition to a world without Dallin in it wouldn't be so jarring. It's a miracle to have family that understands what you need in the moment when you need it most.

And speaking of understanding, that was another miracle that came to me as I sought it.

I asked my school and church communities to give me twenty-four hours of no contact after we came home from the hospital. Immediately, my phone went silent, and I had a whole day of blessed peace and recovery. It might not sound like much, but it was enough that, going forward, I could greet people without punching them in the face or throwing my phone against the wall. Plus, those who cared most about me also got some useful insight about me: that I'm the type of person who needs some space when things are really bad. They wouldn't have known that if I hadn't asked for what I needed. People are often much more unselfish and resilient than we give them credit for. No one was hurt or offended by my request. They understood.

The first Sunday after Dallin's accident, Tim and I didn't feel up to going to church, so we stayed home. We asked others to step in and handle our various church duties and responsibilities for a while. People didn't judge us about it. They understood.

I have said no to a lot of invitations and social engagements since Dallin died. I frequently slip in and out of rooms full of people I know without stopping to say hi. No one has unfriended me because of it. Everyone understands.

The first day I tried getting back to my regular morning exercise routine, I had to stop halfway through and sit on the floor and cry for a while. My most anxious, sensitive daughter came over and just held me while I cried. She didn't ask questions; she didn't have a panic attack as she is prone to do in stressful times. She was just there for me. She understood.

And every night when I tell my Heavenly Father how sad I am, how empty I feel, how angry it makes me that all this is happening to us, He doesn't give me a lecture or make me feel bad. He just listens. Because He understands. And Jesus understands. They always will.

14
The Miracle of Memories

One of the biggest jobs that fell to me in the week after Dallin died was putting together the slideshow that would play in the church foyer during the viewing. It was one of those jobs that's healing and horrible at the same time. I never knew which emotion would hit me the hardest each time I sat down to tackle it.

The hard thing about compiling a life's worth of memories into one thirty-minute video loop is coming to terms with the fact that memories are all we have from now on. For the rest of this life, there will be no new birthdays, no new holidays, no new accomplishments, no new failures. The memories we have are the ones we'll have to get by on. That is a gut-wrenching truth to have to acknowledge. I don't think I'll ever be done crying about it.

The great thing for me about going through that slideshow process was realizing how many things we got to experience with Dallin during his short life. Just looking back at this last year—our last year together—it's amazing the number of great memories we have to treasure.

Dallin started learning Portuguese at school. I speak two foreign languages and Tim speaks three, and we've always felt kind of guilty that we didn't raise our kids to be bilingual. The opportunity Dallin had to get just the basics of conversation and pronunciation down were really special, especially since Tim was a missionary in Brazil. He coached Dallin on how to pray in Portuguese, they would have little conversations about how his day was or what chores he was supposed to be doing, and they would snuggle on the couch reading the Book of Mormon together, an English copy in one hand and a Portuguese copy in the other.

At the end of second grade, Dallin's class hatched chicks, and he was over the moon about it. On the days that I substitute taught a class at his school, he would drag me over to his classroom at the end of the day to make sure I could adequately appreciate how awesome and adorable they were. I've never seen him so gentle as when he tenderly cradled those chicks in his little hands.

I got to substitute teach his class at school several times and chaperone his second-grade field trip to the zoo. For Dallin's classmates who showed up to the funeral, I think it was helpful that I was a familiar face.

Tim took him to his first and only trip to an actual barber shop. He felt so grown up sitting in the chair while the barber worked the clippers, getting his hair styled with gel when the cut was done.

In the spring of 2022, Dallin tried out for a competitive soccer league. He didn't make the A team, but there was interest in forming a B team. I wasn't sure whether or not to sign him up. These teams practice and compete all year round, and they are expensive and time-consuming. Dallin liked to play soccer, but he wasn't a standout athlete, and he wasn't as devoted to the sport as some other kids his age. However, I felt inspired to sign him up.

The first couple weeks were tough, and Dallin got tired. At one point, he even asked if he could quit. But the uniforms had been ordered, the fees had been paid, and I told him that he needed to stick it out for one year to give his body a chance to get strong and see if he might grow to love it. He persevered, and he found the joy that comes after the hard. He loved playing soccer with his friends. He learned to push himself and hustle up and down the field right up until the end of the game. He learned to find value in playing with all his heart and in improving his skills, even when his team lost, which they did more often than not. And he learned to be a part of a team, to value and be kind to each member, and to see himself as part of a unit that could do more together than any of them could do alone. I'll forever be grateful to his coaches and teammates. I know he'll take those lessons with him and that they'll serve him well in the work he does beyond the veil.

We started teaching Dallin to play Dungeons and Dragons. He named his character Adrik Dankill because he liked how all the letters of his name were in it but mixed up.

Over the summer, my parents bought him a new bike, and he spent almost every day until school started riding around the neighborhood, drifting from one friend's house to the next. It was amazing to see him suddenly take on that new level of independence.

We got summer passes to a local amusement park. It's not the kind of thing I usually splurge on, as I'm the stingy one in my marriage. But Dallin had never ridden a roller coaster in his life, and I thought it was time. I'll never forget the look of pure joy on his face when he came rushing off the first ride, bursting to tell us how amazing it had been.

One day, Tim took Dallin with him when he went four-wheeling with friends. They had a great time, especially when Tim let Dallin take a turn with the steering. (He assures me it was during a calm stretch of road, and it was all very safe.) They were in an out-of-the-way spot with no bathrooms, and at one point, Dallin had to go to the bathroom (number two). He got very stressed out about how he would handle this unfamiliar situation, but Tim used his signature calm and showed him how to be a responsible outdoorsman. He dug a hole, showing Dallin how big and how deep it should be. Dallin took care of business, and they filled the hole back in with dirt. My son was so excited and proud that he dragged his cousin over to the spot to show off his workmanship and brag to him about his new survival skills.

Dallin got baptized and confirmed a member of The Church of Jesus Christ of Latter-day Saints in August, shortly after his eighth birthday. He took that ordinance very seriously, and when the bishop interviewed him beforehand to make sure he was ready, I was blown away by how much he understood about the promises he was making to God. Dallin made lots of mistakes, for sure, and he didn't always remember to be kind, but he truly wanted to be a good person. The same cousin who was with him during his four-wheeling adventure, who wasn't sure at the time whether he wanted to be baptized, decided to get baptized after attending Dallin's baptism.

Dallin and his teacher at church shared a love of Reese's Peanut Butter Cups. She would often bring some to class to share with the kids. When Dallin got a special birthday pack of Reese's one Sunday, he went to his seat and offered one to her right away. She tried to refuse, saying that it was his birthday present. But he insisted, saying he wanted her to have one because he knew she loved them just as much as he did.

He finished all the books in the *How to Train Your Dragon* series. He loved giggling over the silly character names and the mild potty humor in those stories and would often read little snippets out loud to me as he read in the morning while eating breakfast.

Dallin perfected what came to be known as his crab walk. It was his signature move. Wherever he was, he would drop to the ground, put both feet behind his head, and scoot around on his bottom using his hands to propel himself forward. It was his favorite way to introduce himself to a new friend.

At Halloween, he carved a pumpkin almost all by himself for the first time. He picked out the design, scraped out the seeds, and carefully maneuvered the little pumpkin carving saw along the lines I had sketched out for him. He was so proud to pose with it as I snapped photos of the finished product.

When winter came, Dallin helped me shovel snow off the driveway, and he went sledding for the first time on sleds my parents bought us for Christmas.

He went with Tim to the Macey's grocery store and got a gigantic soft-serve ice cream cone one evening after he finished his homework.

But most of Dallin's time was spent making friends and telling jokes. He loved to be silly, he loved getting attention, and he loved making people laugh. Almost all of the notes we received from his classmates talked about how funny he was. His closest friends even complained that when they played Fortnite together, Dallin would make them laugh so hard that they would make a mistake, costing them the game. Dallin also liked winning.

Then, of course, there was Christmas. Way back when COVID hit and everyone was on lockdown, my kids started making home movies to fill the long hours of isolation. When December 2020 rolled around, we decided to make short musical videos for the twelve days of Christmas that we could post on Facebook. This would be a sort of family concert done in episodes. It would give my kids performance experience and bring a bit of cheer to anyone feeling lonely and dismal at the end of such a stressful year. I enjoyed doing it so much that we did it again in 2021, this time with a Star Wars Christmas theme.

For 2022, my kids had their own brilliant idea for a theme. There's a YouTube channel they are quite fond of called Good Mythical Morning. The hosts of that show, Rhett and Link, have put out a couple albums of comical songs, and my kids love them beyond reason. They decided that we should do "Twelve Days of Mythical Christmas," with Christmas-themed parodies of Rhett and Link's songs and shows. It was a great idea. And it was going to be a lot of work.

All year long I planned on doing this project, but things came up in our busy lives, and when the holiday season rolled around, I still hadn't really made any progress. I almost gave it up. But a very clear, very strong spiritual prompting told me that this was important. This was not just another gingerbread house we would spend way too much time on and then toss in the garbage can. Something about this project was urgent and weighty, and I had to see it through.

I wrote the words, arranged the music, directed and edited the videos, hassled my husband for help on the technical stuff, and we got it done. Barely. And now we have a beautiful memory: our last home video project for our last Christmas all together. There were recordings of Dallin singing, footage of him destroying a snowman with a baseball bat, a visual record of all his goofing around and harassing his sisters and ignoring my direction and throwing a fit when he didn't win some silly game. Just him. We got it all on film one last time. What a miracle.

Now that Dallin is gone, I can't imagine not having those silly Christmas videos. I can't imagine the regret I would have felt if I had followed my first impulse and said, "I don't have enough energy. We don't really have the time. Maybe next year." Because there *was* no next year. God knew it, and He let me know what I needed to do even though He couldn't tell me why. Through His tender mercies, we have beautiful last experiences and memories to cherish. And even when it hurts to look at the pictures and watch the videos, they will always remind us that Dallin lived a full life, even if it wasn't full-term.

15
The Miracle of Grief

No matter how much we resist it, life goes back to its normal rhythm after the death of a loved one. It happens far too quickly, and it feels wrong in every way.

It starts with small things. One day after the funeral was over and all my sisters had gone home, I went to pick up my youngest daughter from elementary school for the first time since the accident. I hadn't realized that I had been avoiding that task until I saw the first little boy bounding out of the back gate, and I was overwhelmed by the realization that it would never be Dallin. Never again.

A short time after that, I went grocery shopping at Walmart. I had to walk past the boys clothing section and saw a pair of camouflage pants that were very similar to the ones Dallin wore his last day on earth. They were his favorite. There in the store, I flashed back to a memory of the first responders cutting those pants off of him on the playground as they treated him. I remembered thinking, "I'll have to try to find some replacement pants that he likes just as well when this is all over." It hit me very hard that day that that would no longer be necessary, and it broke my heart.

Another time, a neighbor brought us ice cream sandwiches for a treat, and I had to divide them equally between all the members of our family. I caught myself dividing the total by six instead of five. How I wished I could go without dessert for the rest of my life so I could give all the extras to Dallin. All these little "normal" things were so painful in so many unexpected ways that I just wanted to crawl under my covers and pretend the world would go away if only I ignored it with enough determination.

But life will not stop for us. Kids have school assignments to complete, parents have bills to pay, and dishes will only sit in the sink so long before they start to mold. So we pull ourselves together and do the hard work of figuring out how to muddle through the duties of daily life when nothing will ever be okay again.

And it's true. For the rest of my life, I will always and at every moment be profoundly not okay.

But that's not all I will be.

We look at a mountain, and we know that it's never just one thing. The snow-capped peaks, the lush forested patches, the hidden caves, the rugged cliffs—they are all a part of what makes up the whole. One part of the mountain doesn't limit what the other parts can be. They coexist as a symbiotic ecosystem that bring beauty and wonder to our world.

We are the same.

The grief that I feel doesn't limit my ability to feel joy, and being joyful isn't disloyal to the memory of the one I have lost. I will miss my son with every breath that I take, with every beat of my heart, but that part of me will not define my whole self. I can be mournful *and* joyful, regretful *and* hopeful, somber *and* silly. Profound emotion increases our emotional capacity in both directions. That's why losing the ones we love most causes us the most suffering. And it's why faith will not take away our sadness. God intends us to be like Him. And He is not limited in His capacity to feel.

As we increase our emotional range through the experiences of mortality, we come to understand the nature of our Heavenly Father more completely. How He can love us so fiercely as His children yet sorrow so deeply because of our wickedness. How He can be the God of the Old Testament, full of wrathful threatenings and prophecies of vengeance, and also be the God of the New Testament, preaching at all times forgiveness, compassion, long-suffering, and healing. One part of Him does not define the whole. But to see the whole, we must gain experience with the parts, even when it hurts. He will help us.

Just as our Savior strengthens us through our greatest trials, He also enlarges us through our greatest suffering. He knows what grief can do for us, so He will not take it away. His Atonement opens our hearts through our grief so we can feel more and be more. It makes our whole emotional selves greater than the sum of our parts. As Elder Neil A. Maxwell once said, "The cavity which suffering carves into our souls will one day also be the receptacle of joy."[17] This means that when we are yoked with the Savior, we don't need to be afraid of the mountain. It brings us to a higher place.

Jesus taught us these truths by how He reacted to the death of His friend Lazarus. In the scriptures, we read that Lazarus's sisters, Mary and Martha, summon Jesus to their home in Bethany in order to heal their brother, who has fallen ill. But when Jesus finally arrives, Lazarus is dead. In fact, he has "lain in the grave four days already" (John 11:17). Mary and Martha rush to meet Jesus, bemoaning the fact that He didn't get there in time to save their brother but expressing faith in His divine power. Then, when Jesus goes to Lazarus's grave, He weeps (see John 11:35).

Now, it's no surprise to Jesus that Lazarus is dead. In fact, just a few verses earlier, He informs His disciples of this fact before they even begin their journey to Bethany. He says, "I am glad for your sakes that I was not there, to the intent ye may believe" (John 11:14). The Savior intentionally waits until after Lazarus dies to go to him. He knows this will be the perfect opportunity to show His disciples that He truly is the Messiah, with power over death, and to give them a foreshadowing of His own death and Resurrection that will come in the near future. He has hope and a perfect knowledge that everything will be okay.

Yet He weeps.

Christ's joy in what is to come does not limit His ability or His need to grieve the loss of His friend. His whole emotional capacity extends beyond the parts, yet He takes time to honor each part by pausing to weep before He moves on to the happy ending. Jesus doesn't heal Lazarus because He is afraid of death or the sorrow that comes with it. His heart is big enough for all the feelings, and He makes room

---

17. Neal A. Maxwell, "But for a Small Moment" (Brigham Young University devotional, Sept. 1, 1974), 3, speeches.byu.edu.

for each of them. He can help us be like Him. I have faith that He will help me be like Him—that my faith in Him will make me more.

So from now on, when people who care about me ask with worried expressions and genuine love how I am, I won't have just one answer. I will have to reply that, in all honesty, I am terrible. To some degree, I will be doing terrible until the day my family is reunited in heaven. But I will also say that, in all honesty, I am doing well—that I am finding peace and making new memories that fill the cavity in my soul with joy. I am coming to see that Dallin's death has changed me, but it will not limit me.

Because of my Savior, my grief will not constrict me—it will enlarge me. It will not destroy me—it will sanctify me. My sorrow will bind me more fully to my Heavenly Father and to those I love on both sides of the veil. It will empower me to have room in my heart for all the feelings so that I can love more fully and hope more steadfastly and empathize more sincerely. It will make me more like God. That is the miracle of grief.

16
The Miracle of Covenants

A FEW MONTHS AFTER DALLIN'S DEATH, I SAT IN CHURCH AS A STALwart and venerable lady came to the pulpit to address the congregation. She is a woman of incredible strength whose life has been filled with service and devotion to the Lord. She said how grateful she was to live in this beautiful valley and that she hoped we would all be blessed to know what we have. I've thought about her words a lot since then as I've contemplated the actual valley where I live and written about the metaphorical valley that I'm wading through.

As I recount the miracles that have blessed me since the passing of my son, I've come to understand that the valley truly is beautiful. Stunning vistas, majestic peaks, shimmering lakes, meadows sprinkled with daffodils—all of these and more make this valley we share a vision of loveliness. But when the shadow of death falls over us, it's hard to see that beauty. There's so much darkness, and it extends in all directions as far as we can see. It feels like it will never be over. Even when we remember that we used to see beautiful things, we are so sad and depressed and hopeless and angry that the memory isn't enough to make us able to see them again. It's just so dark. It's just so hard.

We need help to see the beauty. We need help to see the miracles.

In The Church of Jesus Christ of Latter-day Saints, we talk a lot about covenants. We call ourselves the covenant people of the Lord. In simplest terms, what this means is that we make promises to God, and He makes promises to us in return. It's not so much a contract as a bond, bringing to mind the New Testament imagery of the bridegroom calling his people to the wedding feast (see Matthew 25). When we make covenants with the Lord, we take His name upon us, like a bride takes the name of her husband after they are married. We belong to each other, and His ability to help us increases. As His name becomes our name, so His strength becomes our strength and His eyes become our eyes. As we keep our covenants consistently over time, our bond grows stronger and our vision grows clearer.

The night my family came home from the hospital with one fewer person than we should have had, Tim and I fell quickly into a troubled sleep. I woke up at around 4:00 in the morning, wide awake, with words in my head that needed to be written. Though we hadn't even started planning Dallin's funeral, I knew with sudden urgency that I had to be the one speak at it, and I knew the things I needed to say. I sat in our front room and wrote as the sun rose slowly over the mountains of the Tooele Valley, and the Holy Ghost gave me the message that would bring peace to me and to all who came to mourn with us on the day we would publicly lay Dallin to rest. In that space, with the room so quiet and the Spirit so near, I felt the shadow recede from my soul just a little bit. Just for a moment.

This book is an expansion of that talk. It is an assurance from God that He has answered my prayers and kept His promises. I went into the shadow expecting miracles, and they came in abundance. Like the disciples who went fishing at the sea of Tiberias following Jesus's crucifixion, I cast my net and was "not able to draw it for the multitude of fishes" (John 21:6).

Most of the miracles I've written about here are ones I wouldn't have seen if I hadn't been looking for them. The act of seeking and expecting miracles is really just a variation on a doctrinal theme as old as Adam and Eve: exercising faith. The Lord can't open our eyes to see if we don't have faith that He will. We have to believe in Him before He can show us how hard He's working to send us the miracles we need.

And yet it seems awfully unfair to expect us to believe in God at times like these. All the evidence of the moment seems to disprove our faith. When someone dies as suddenly as Dallin did in a way that seems so senseless, it's easy to lose your footing, spiritually speaking. If the question of life and death truly hinges on the whims of fate, on something as heartless and meaningless as chance and coincidence, how can we believe that our lives mean anything? That we are of any significance in the boundless void of eternity? In the vast emptiness of space and time, doesn't every accidental death prove that we are nothing? That our lives matter as little as the dust we shake off our feet or the wave that crashes on the beach and disappears back into the ocean?

I say no.

The story is told of a man who, while hiking across a glacier, fell through the ice. Luckily for him, he was anchored to a solid piece of ground behind him and had an able-bodied hiking buddy who could pull him up to safety. Our anchor is Christ. The rope that binds us to Him and holds us when we fall is our covenants. Many people wonder why we have so many rules in the Church—so many restrictions and so many time-consuming responsibilities. We are exercising faith by building a covenant life. Every time we keep a promise we have made to the Lord, the cord that binds us to Him gets a little stronger. And after years of keeping those promises, that cord turns to steel so strong that when our world falls apart around us, we are held firm. The stronger the covenant life we have built, the firmer our faith will remain, and the more clearly we will see that God is in the details of our lives and that there are legions of angels rushing to our aid. We don't develop the faith to see the miracles in the moment we need them. That is the work of a lifetime.

As I have previously said, my life has not been a series of random events. Every moment has been carefully crafted so that when I got to this point—to the day when my world fell apart as God knew it would—I would have the tools I needed to get through it. What I have realized is that the greatest preparation I received was in my own hands the whole time. I made covenants and never stopped trying to keep them, despite my many failings and shortcomings. And that has made all the difference. I am amazed at the great work that God has been able to bring to pass in my life. Even knowing that He is God, with infinite knowledge, perspective, and power, I still manage to be surprised by all He is able to do for us. My life is a witness that it is not all chaos and anarchy. I prepared myself to be close to Him by building a relationship with Him, and He showed me that there is order and meaning to the whole, even when this part of our experience is a cruel twist of fate that hinges on the accident of a moment.

Of course, not everyone will be blessed in the same ways that my family has been blessed in our day of great suffering. Not everyone lives in an environment where their religious beliefs are understood and respected so completely and unquestioningly. Not everyone will have a community with the will and resources to rally around them as generously as ours has. Not everyone will have a friend who can handle the press, siblings who can rush to their side, or music to soothe their broken heart. Many people don't even get the chance to say a proper goodbye to the one who leaves them. I know it's hard not to feel cheated when you don't get the miracles you expected, or even the ones you feel like you need to make it through the day. It's not fair. And I'm sorry if, in telling you about my blessings, I've increased your pain. Please forgive me.

But I stand by the promise of miracles.

Building a covenant life can start on any day, at any point in your life. And the minute you start to exercise the particle of faith it takes to make and keep promises to the Lord, His ability to work miracles in your life increases. At the same time, your ability to perceive the miracles that He has already sent you increases as well. It's dark in the valley when the shadow descends, and we can't see without His light. None of us can. Alone, we will wander off, fall away into forbidden paths, and be lost (see 1 Nephi 8:23, 28). It's easy to lose yourself to grief. We need help to see our way through. That way will be unique to each of us because the miracles God sends us are unique to our needs and situations.

As President Nelson said, "The Lord does not require perfect faith for us to have access to His perfect power. But He does ask us to believe."[18] Jesus Christ promises that through our faith, He will grant us the power to move mountains (see Matthew 17:20). But death is a mountain that will not be moved, no matter how much faith we have. As hard as it is to comprehend, what we need most is not the power to live forever in this world with the people we love. This world is not the final destination—not the paradise we dreamed of when we agreed to

18. Russell M. Nelson, "Christ Is Risen; Faith in Him Will Move Mountains," *Liahona*, May 2021, 102.

invest in the risky enterprise of mortality. What we truly need is vision to see the mountain for what it is: a part of His plan—an essential part of His plan, in fact. It's not a barrier or an obstacle or a curse. It's a seamless extension of our beautiful valley, and the path that leads there is our way home. May we all be blessed to see the beauty of the valley. May we all have access to the vision and power of God to know what we have.

17
Walking through the Valley

Perhaps you think it pretentious of me to write a book about grief so soon after the passing of my son. Living with loss for a few months certainly doesn't make me an expert on the subject. Maybe I should have waited until time and distance had given me perspective and experience—until I had a chance to see how grief would hit me in new and unexpected ways as the months and years roll on. After all, we haven't even celebrated his next birthday, our first Christmas without him, or the first anniversary of his death. Who knows how those events will affect me, or how they will affect each one of us in our family and in the community. Maybe I should have waited.

But there's something special about the things you learn at the beginning of a journey. There's a freshness to the pain you endure but also an energy you give to enduring it that aren't quite replicable after time and miles have worn you down and made you wise. Because the revelations I have received during this first phase of my grief have come so powerfully and in such great numbers, I was afraid they would fade and grow dim before I had a chance to preserve them. I wanted to remember, so I wrote. I felt I could help someone, so I'm sharing.

The truth is, we're all in the valley. We all have to make our peace with the mountain. We all have to negotiate the consequences of the shadow it casts. Nothing can change that—not shutting our eyes, not running away, not finding a dark cave to hide in. So I will walk through this valley of shadow, looking up for the sunrise and finding pockets of warmth along the way. And in the days when the shadows are darkest, I will rest in the knowledge that the sun will shine on me again. And though I am sad, though I am weary, "yea, though I walk through the valley of the shadow of death, I will fear no evil: for thou art with me; thy rod and thy staff they comfort me" (Psalm 23:4).

We all have hard days and years ahead of us as we try to cope with the consequences of Dallin's passing. We can't even know yet how hard they will be. I wish to heaven we could have been spared it. But through the power of God and His Son, Jesus Christ, we can expect miracles. They will come to us if we seek them.

About the Author

Kathryn Cunningham was always the kid with a story to tell. As a mother, as a teacher, and as a friend, she is always at her best when there's a story involved. She has gathered her stories and honed her skills as a French major at BYU, a proselyting missionary in Germany, a military wife in Korea and Germany, a member of the writing team for the refugee advocacy organization TSOS (Their Story Is Our Story), a stay-at-home mom and CEO of her family all over the USA, and the list goes on. She never dreamed that one day she'd have to tell the story of how she lost her son, but she's grateful for the experiences, the mentors, and the gospel truths that have prepared her to do it.

Scan to visit

www.kathryncunninghamauthor.com